I0528536

A Map
Without
Your Shadow

poetry by Kat Heatherington

ECHOBIRD
PRESS

Address inquiries in permission to:
Echobird Press, echobirdpress.com
ISBN 978-1-931370-02-9 | ISBN 978-1-961370-03-6 EPUB

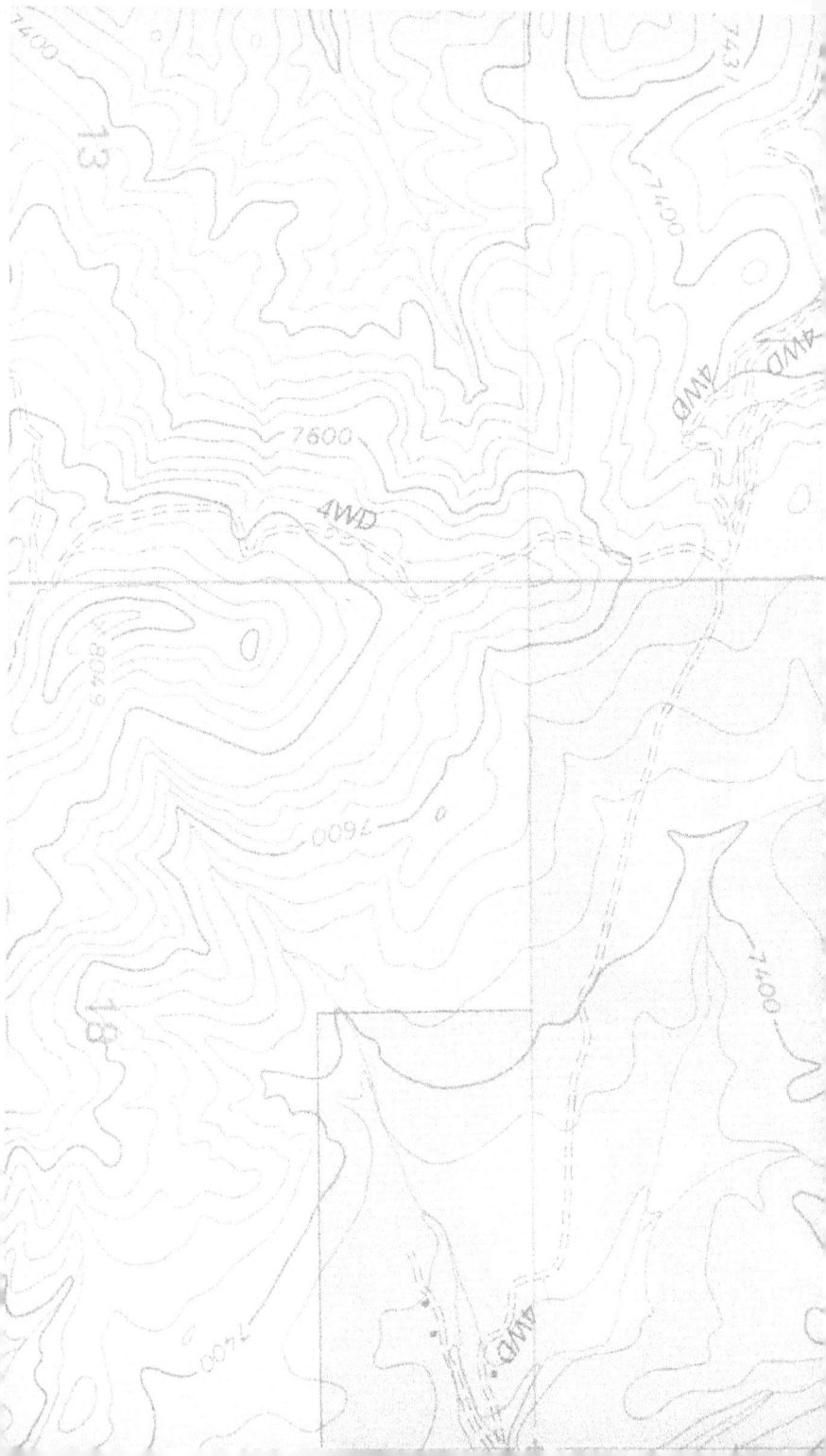

Table of Contents

Compass Rose —

rock

your lines are crisp, your heart
steady. you don't blur
easily into poetry.
but every time i falter,
or need some safe place to lean,
my rock, you're there.

a little questioning

i'm not seeing fireworks,
or feeling dragonflies of certainty,
but i sure am in love.
this love is gentle and steady
and patient and strong
as often as it's whimsical and
sexy and leaves me laughing
so hard i recur into giggles for hours.
it catches me smiling at odd moments,
and saying odd things.
excess certainty always
gets me in trouble anyhow—
when i'm most certain,
i tend to be most wrong.
a little doubt, a little questioning,
clears the air.
there's more to love
in uncertainty resolved,
than in the definite answer
that never thinks to ask.

the river still runs through us

two houses and a thousand miles later
the river still runs through us.
cranesong in the early morning,
cracking the soft light.
the shifting waters of the well
beneath the house, the way land
moves under those who steward it
grows and dies back, and grows again.

the things we don't say

lights on both sides of the river, now.
not enough darkness anywhere.
airport towers flash red to the silent night
thin air heavy with drought
and the things we don't say.
unseen signals flash past the averted gaze,
the swallowed thought.
red in the silent night,
the moving water unlit, black,
between the riverbanks.

fall any faster

i wish i could see in the dark,
see through whatever it is that lies between us.
you tell me i'm not falling fast enough.
i'm doing everything i can to live right,
to bring our agreed-upon dreams to life.
all of a sudden, that's not enough.
i'm not doing it right.
i can't meet this demand and
be everything else i've committed to being,
do everything i need to do.
i can't fall any faster
without coming apart.

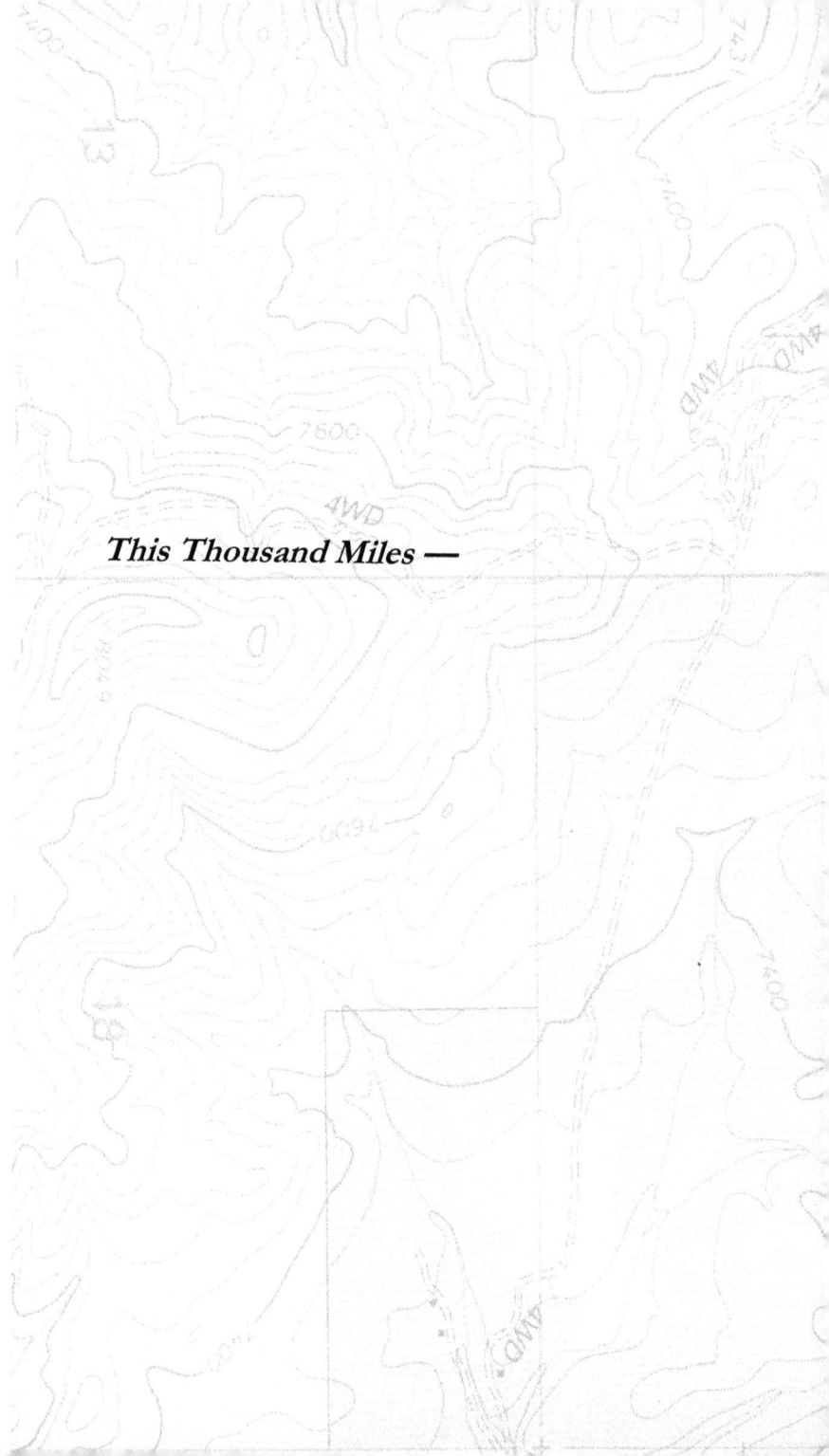

This Thousand Miles —

an apple dipped in honey

an apple dipped in honey for the turning year.
a handgun i can't use locked up below the shelf.
the quiet rush of intermittent water in the pond.
yellow leaves falling, everywhere falling.
drifts pile beside the doors,
leaves skirl in small wind.
each breath of air brings a patter on the roof.
books boxed into the attic, a fire in the hearth.
one cat asleep by my thigh, the other
on your doorstep, loudly missing you.
over and over and over he cries:
a thousand miles lie between us.
what is an apple dipped in honey,
next to that?

the wrong light

the light coming up behind me
is not your light. wintering
fields lie to all sides,
dark as pools of water,
this rich, uneven ground.
each light flickers, steadies,
and floods past.
you could drown
in the dark of those fields.
better than drowning
in the wrong light.

the heat of this night

i stand in a twilit field
watching the water ease in,
watching flickering bats hunt mosquitoes,
watching you prepare to leave again.
the water seeps over dry soil,
finds every fissure, pours in.
the bat careens in circles,
appearing and disappearing against a darkening sky,
feasting and frantic.
you load the last boxes into your truck,
shut the tailgate, and meet my eyes.
it will be half a year
before you return.
the last light slips from the sky.
at least, this time, it is summer.
the heat of this night must hold me
until you return.

summer tanager

a summer tanager trills in the dusk,
bright, invisible bird
deep in the leafy canopy
of incoming autumn.
over and over he calls,
love me, love this
strangely misty sunset, love
these trees, this beautiful
hard-working farm.
over and over i reply, i do —
i do love this little red bird,
and each of these things,
this place in its wholeness,
but all i can feel is alone
in a deepening twilight
that aims itself toward
another winter without you
here, celebrating, loving and
working this small farm
by my side.

Uncharted —

what has changed

this rain and i are both fatigued
slow, soft around the edges.
a little cold for the season.
so much is easier when you are not here.
so much is difficult because you are not here.
we said this is forever.
we said, "you and me, we've got this. always."
a thousand miles echo between us,
undulating like a sine wave,
necessary and impossible.
it is changing us.
it is too early, yet, to see
what it has changed.

love is not enough

i love you, you say, over again
till it becomes a wall.
a defense, an excuse, where
there are no other defenses, excuses.
but surely you have learned by now
that love is not enough.

litter

a flock of small birds
litters the sky, and is gone.
a girl you say you're not dating
is allowed to stay the whole day,
and i turn up the music
to drown out her laughter,
which echoes. frost finally
takes down the tomato vines,
fruit falling soft on earth
covered over with cottonwood leaves,
gold and browning.
rain fails to fall.
i want to believe she's
good for you, but the girl
leaves tension in her wake –
you can't reclaim your day,
and i can't give you my evening.
all night, dry leaves
rain down from crystal-clear heavens,
this season's only fruit.

taillights

you drive away from me
and into a storm,
headwind blowing you south & east
all the long day.
you sleep in your bed by the ocean that night,
farthest west, nevertheless.
part of my soul stands still
in that parking lot, watching
your taillights turn the corner,
and disappear.
i don't yet know all the ways
we have changed and are changing.
i only wish you could stop leaving
so we could find out.

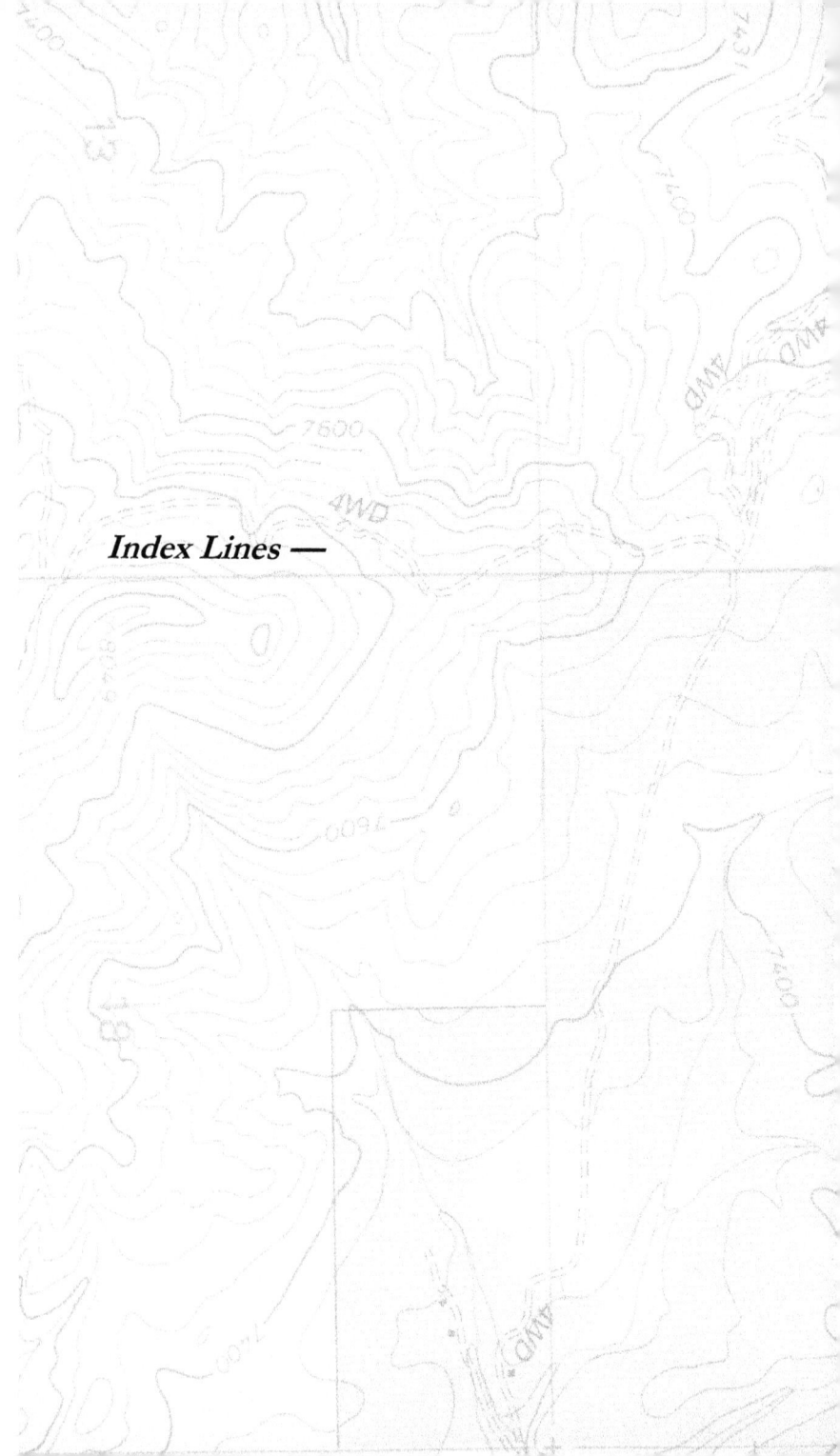

Index Lines —

the scent of shattering

the night smells like ice,
not rain, but the scent
of shattering.
what could have been
and wasn't. isn't.
the breaking, at the end
of a long road,
no longer together,
no longer mutual,
no longer infused with care.
something that we have built, breaking.
something that has been building,
collapsing under its own weight.
a crack, a rift, a canyon, an abyss.
you recede on the far shore.
you have been receeding
longer than i have been willing
to admit it.
it is time to finish falling.
and see what remains.

untangling

i am untangling necklaces,
as if by doing so i could untangle my life -
an act of sympathetic magic
so complete it would tease apart the strands
of childhood and history,
of expectation and abandonment,
of stubborn strength and fierce pride
until the weave that led to you is unwoven.
the web that led me to choose you and then
to keep choosing you when unease
ripped through me in sucking waves
and i went to bed wondering if i had married an alien
(i did not let myself think the word: monster) -
when people i loved drew back from you
and said nothing to me -
when you did real harm in home and community
spoke unforgivable words
chose and repeated unforgivable acts --
even when a friend said, "of course
abusers are charming, that's how they get you,"
and "the fact that it's intermittent
is part of what makes it abuse" --
still i chose you, and stubbornly stuck
like a foxtail seed,
to what i had chosen.
to the good parts, that shrank
to good memories and then
to memories haunted by shame
and self-recrimination.
now i would untangle the whole pattern,
weft and warp entire, and weave anew
a shape that would let me
see red flags and heed them,
listen when your actions told me who you were

in spite of your words and in defiance of them,
and act when it was clear
that inaction was drowning
in the riptide of unease;
that inaction was wrong.
now i separate fine chains and chunky stones,
polished smooth, turquoise and jasper
gleaming in soft evening light
and i lay them straight beside one another on the bed, tidy.
i have arrived in this place, this seeing.
i am weaving a new pattern now.

the day after i asked for a divorce

woke up and cried bitterly
half an hour.
relief and grief are twins.
made spreadsheets,
paid bills,
briefly despaired.
then forced myself to rally.
there will be a way through
because there must be.
one small miracle
is all it will take.
surely that
is not too
much to ask.
thought about calling mom,
reconsidered, decided
to await the next development.
waiting is the hardest part.
it would be a grievous error
to crowd him,
to rush the process.
the stakes
are too high for
foolish mistakes.
so don't make them.
make tea, instead,
pet the cat.
take the time to be grateful
he's letting you
keep the cat.
soon, there will be no more "letting."
no more waiting.
soon, you will be your own person,
entire,

free as you have never
wholly been before.
never again to lock
the manacle of a wedding band
around your ambitions.
it is worth grieving the marriage.
and worth waiting
for the arrival
of your wholeness.

work i don't want to do

you are work i don't want to do.
i'd rather run up the steps
at my own pace, intuitive, leaping,
instead of having to backtrack to bring you along,
not even one stairstep at a time,
and that with great labor.
if it weren't for the farm,
for these detailed and specific circumstances,
i'd leave you behind,
let you puzzle it out, or not,
in your own glacial time.
"glacial" is exact.
(you like exactitude.)
you grind down everything in your path,
flatten mountains and carve lakes
where they stood, when you can.
you are relentless.
this does not mean you are correct.
in wearing down mountains,
you rely on your deep slowness –
it exhausts the opposition.
i never wanted to become
the opposition.
when we were harnessed to the same plow,
we could, and often did,
do anything we set our minds to.
but i have kept moving in the same direction
and you have set yourself
opposite me. you are probably hoping
to wear me down.
i will not be so worn.
i will not let you grind me into morraine.
i will run up the steps without you,
and if you do not follow,
i will be gone.

escape

it is not marshland i'm escaping this time
but a cold and stony wasteland
where there used to be a garden.
oh, there were always stony outcrops,
but what garden doesn't have those?
they were easy to explain away.
but slowly as the years wound by,
the flowers wilted, then stopped
blooming altogether, the vegetables
produced less and less every year and
barren patches grew around the outcrops,
until there was only a thin wind
stipping the soil away, layer by layer.
a thin wind, and sometimes,
a lightning storm. it has gone
beyond any explanation or excuse.
now there is only an angry man
pretending to be a kind man,
saying, *obviously, i love you. i still
pay the bills.* obviously. the only
obvious thing here is that it is time
for me to leave.

taking out the trash

four and a half years of lies
four and a half years of sweeping it
under the rug.
of choosing to ignore
the uncomfortable.
of focusing on the good
while the harm festered.
i am taking all the rugs to the laundry.
i am getting rid of rugs.
anything that cannot meet my eyes
in the cold light of day
cannot live in my house.

the light you left behind, reprise

to remember him as a man
is to remember a wound.
the mind skips over it, lemon juice in an open cut,
let's not. hopscotch to any other thought.
you remember making love with him,
years ago, the shape of his body in the lamplight,
delight and satisfaction and the certainty
that things would work out.
they have certainly worked out, but
you flinch from the memory
as you came to flinch from his touch.
first reluctance, grudging acceptance,
a necessary chore – to keep the peace,
be touched by this man you used to love.
easy enough to tolerate. then
active resistance, the arrival of your No.
excuses, negotiations. by then
it was all negotiation and no love song.
by the end, reluctance and resistance
expanded into revulsion.
the very thought brought a shudder,
a coiling inwards, a step back.
how dare you lay a hand on me.
he mostly didn't. only words.
now you probe fourteen years of memory
with a delicate hand, rummaging,
turning over small moments,
looking for the light you, he, left behind.
it is there.
it is well and truly past, paved over by change,
betrayal, and resentment, but it is there.
you did not waste your youth –
you lived it, fully.
tonight, 45 years old and divorced,

you dye your hair red and spiky,
and tell over the names of all your lovers
like rosary beads in the dark.
he is only one of them.
and it was worth it, every one.
there is much you could wish to change,
but you arrive in this moment without regrets.
knowing your life is only half lived.
the next half unfurls before you,
an unwritten page waiting only
for you to take up the pen.

compost

for the longest time, i swept
every troubling thing you did
under the rug.
it was easy to let slide, at first —
one ugly deed without resolution, then
long sweet months slid by before another.
until years passed and somehow it was all the time,
nothing left but evasion and
mirror-polished hollows and rot.
nothing was easy, by then.
neither confrontation nor evasion.
the middle ground i tried so hard to occupy
had vanished, devoured by the very rug
we stored our secrets under.
our evasions and denials and your lies.
now you are gone and i want
to sweep you under the rug.
there's no man here, there never was a man.
if i do this, i know, the rug will grow lumpy,
fester, then burst out sideways
in a scuttle of legs and hair and slime
at untoward moments.
no. i am getting rid of rugs.
there once was a man here, and a marriage,
and now they are here no more.
i must look every inch of it in the eye,
and turn it over, examine the underside,
make my peace with it,
and fork it into the compost pile
where scuttling legs and slime
break down just as easily
as food scraps and weeds.
i will rot the good out of it.
i will feed this earth
on the debris of that marriage,
break it down to black dirt teeming
with invisible, beneficial life,
and grow tomatoes from what remains.

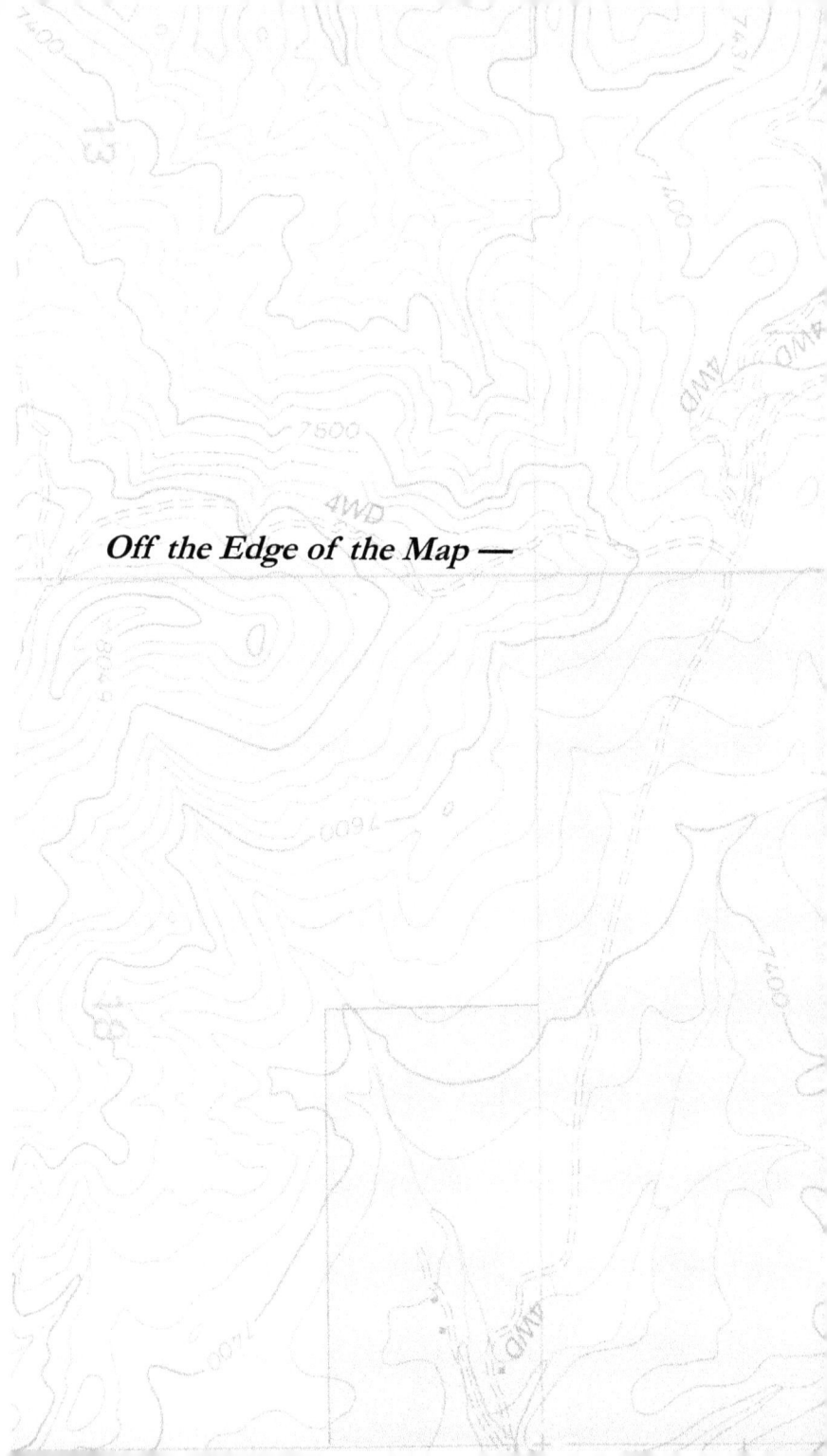

Off the Edge of the Map —

grief is an enzyme

you knew that it could never be the same
you are bitter anyway,
grieving what isn't.

the breaking light

the light breaks, sharp sun
through thin air
the weather breaks
frost filigrees the dying garden,
leaves fall in their daily thousands.
i break with them,
a leaf-fall of grief,
a sharp angle.
somewhere, a thin light
into what comes next.

aftermath

winter brings a kind of haunting.
even a bright clear winter like this,
all blue skies and mild days
and flowers out of season.
the dark arrives early, lingers late,
and lately, lingers.
fears you banished under the busy summer sun
rise anew and blunder around the house.
you bump into them over the coffee,
washing dishes, folding laundry.
you banish them by taking out the trash but
they're back that night,
stretched out on the bed like the cat,
to worry at your sleep.
it doesn't snow, so you can't
hibernate, the world refuses
to stop or even slow down, gathering
speed & intensity in opposition to itself.
to your animal nature, haunted
by honeysuckle in december
and the shadows
of pain you don't want to name,
lest naming call it back.

#NotAllTrucks

one year later, shockwaves still run
through me when i hear his name.
he drove a black truck and i
flinch when i see a black truck while driving.
i look to make sure it's some innocent stranger,
not the worst and most inescapable mistake of my life
bearing down on me in a homicidal rage,
bent on revenge.
it hasn't been yet, and it's been a year,
but i haven't stopped flinching. when
does the rush and heart-stutter, the adrenaline leap
(run run you are not safe)
leave the body? how long does it take
to feel safe in your own skin all the time again?
even most of the time.
here i am trying to date and still flinching.
i have the idea a new person, new patterns
could help me heal.
i have the idea i need more time.
i'm tired of the flutter and stutter of fear
trembling around me.
it's free-floating, sticks to everything.
there's no task that doesn't
make me anxious, now.
i'd lay that at his feet –
i stopped knowing how to trust myself,
because of what he did to me –
but i don't really want to think of him at all.
i have the idea that
starting from where i am,
rather than reaching backwards,
will be more effective.
most black trucks, after all,
are someone else's.

a map without your shadow

i keep visiting parts of myself
from before i knew you,
making sure i'm still me,
that you haven't broken me.
haven't done irreparable harm.
i journey into the work of repair.
i visit my mother, and old friends from college
and then, not the college itself,
but the mountains that gave shape
to my soul when i lived there.
cicadas and wildflowers,
cascading mountain streams noisy
with cold and ferns and mosses.
manzanita and scrub oak and lilypads.
a young deer in a meadow,
spotted like the flowers.
no. i am wounded but whole,
each place, each person,
a stitch to mend the tear.
each remote dirt road,
an immutable pathway to essential self.
i make sure to take as many new
remote dirt roads as i can find.
i'll stitch a map without your shadow, even.
sewn of maidenhair fern,
old love and new,
and the bones of the Sangre de Cristos.
you fade like a kind of gnawing hunger
into the part of the past we don't talk about.
the clean mountain spring joins the Rio Grande
and waters our fields, feeds
the wildflowers in my own backyard.
every year i plant more of them
until they plant themselves,
and the land sighs relief
in the summer rains,
without even a scar.

trees are made to withstand storms

trees are made to withstand storms
and so are you –
to bend and shake
under the lashing rain and wind,
but also to grow
tall and strong and supple
from that same rain and wind.
many days, lately,
i wake up brittle.
ready to break
where i don't want to bend.
the work is to soften in the right ways,
while staying strong.
the work is to become supple,
not give in to easy bitterness.
to find what i need from this storm
and weather it
and grow.

the day after

he is gone.
he is gone and my spine
is dissolved like butter.
he is gone and a cherry tree
blooms in my garden.
he is gone and the wind
blows dust across dry land
and plays a melody
on the chimes by my door.
he is gone and i have
a lot of cleaning up to do.
he is gone and my house
is safe again.
i am safe again.
he is gone and a long chapter
of my life is closing, has closed.
he is gone and the trees
are leafing out all around.
he is gone and i cannot stop weeping.
he is gone and finally
i can breathe.

the trick

the trick is to heal without hardening.
keep the wound soft
so the scar will be supple.
not to calcify into rigid bitterness
and resignation, but remain,
through it all, open
to the wonder, the delight, the comfort
of every rising sun.

a future i can't envision, but am bolting toward

two months after you finally left –
six months after i asked you to go –
two years after i realized i needed you gone –
i think i should be moving on, starting anew.
case closed, documents filed,
by my hand and seal.
a door propped open,
now firmly shut.
except it seems to bang in the wind,
sometimes in the night.
a cold skirl of air whisks through
at any hour of the day.
i'm over you, but i'm not over it.
i rush headlong into as many
changes as i can absorb, and
i become attached to finishing things –
books, tv series, house projects, the
last of the peanut butter. anything.
each finished task is another clearing,
another opening, a block released.
making space, and more space, and more,
for a future i don't know how to envision,
but am bolting toward.
in it, i will not wake up with a start
in the early dark, heart pounding,
half-convinced and half-terrified
that you are about to walk in and upend
whatever equilibrium i've managed
to cultivate that day.
in it, i will not spend the afternoon
arguing in my head with you,
arguments from years ago,
or new ones, defending, explaining, justifying,
actions i have taken since you left.

since i removed you.
in this unimaginable and desperately longed-for future,
when i am simply safe in my house, body & mind,
i will be absorbed in my present moment,
and will hardly ever think on these months,
this season of sudden change,
and midnight panic attacks,
and how hard it was to let you go
when i so badly needed you gone.

an open space

an open space where my heart used to be.
a vacancy, a void. sudden moonlight.
a field full of stars
sometimes patchy with clouds.
often clear.
a meadow by moonlight, quietly
blossoming.
most days, a garden.
a piece of my heart,
where my heart used to be.

red-winged blackbirds

milkweed and thistle growing wild in the ditches.
a place that is not, and smells like, home.
the wild melody of red-winged blackbirds
skirling and swooping through cattails
by a river still deep with snowmelt.
everything touched by time,
yet wholly itself.
if you look hard enough, you are, too:
touched by time, still singing, still flying,
still yourself.
the shape of this mountain
mirrored in your soul.

rain garden

we built a garden where you used to live.
a path runs right through it,
hard packed after just one week,
crooking slightly, to run in two directions.
when i use it, i feel
like i am walking through your ghost.
i need to grow something beautiful
from what remains of our marriage.
from the ashes of abuse and deceit.
i design a new space,
till the soil, add reams of compost.
i will plant a hundred wildflowers
where you once slept.
and not even one of them
will be your ghost.

without you, anything is possible

crickets and stars and the last yellow slice of the moon.
the night is open, febrile, possible.
without you, i want to do everything at once.
i try to reclaim the lost years,
paint over the history, the pain, the bad decisions
that only came clear in hindsight.
without you, anything can happen.
i open the door wide to the star-strewn darkness,
the leafy heavens, the soft sounds
of midnight in summertime,
scent of rain in the distance.

Acknowledgements

While I am sure I would have survived the experience chronicled in this collection on my own, my life was vastly improved by the care, support, and devotion of Terra McKeown, without whom I would not be the person I am today. I owe a debt of gratitude also to my housemates at Sunflower River, Rev Tsolwizar, Jenny Rice, and Tristan Fin, whose support and material assistance getting out of an emotionally abusive marriage was invaluable. Thank you to everyone who listened, and believed me, and helped me find my way to strength while I was in the thick of it. You made a world of difference. You know who you are.

The manuscript would not be the book it is today, were it not for the insightful and entertaining editorial feedback of Erin Daughtrey. Thank you. None of these poems were previously published – not only because the collection includes new material, but also because the older poems are uncomfortable or unsettling in a way that has led me not to submit them to journals over the years. A pattern I didn't notice until I went through my publication credits to write this note. Interesting.

To everyone who has survived, or is in the act of surviving, an abusive relationship: I see you. You will find a way through. I never thought I would be this person – none of us do – but for all that we each survive alone, in desperation and anger and fear, we also survive together. You've got this.

About the Author

Kat Heatherington is a queer ecofeminist poet, artist, pagan, and organic gardener. Kat's work tackles what one friend memorably described as "stunning transitional moments" – the space between feelings – grief, love, heartbreak, and emotional complexity, threaded through a deep relationship with the natural world. She has several self-published poetry chapbooks, and one book, *The Bones of This Land*, available from the author at yarrowkat@gmail.com and at http://echobirdpress.com.

Her work can be read at https://patreon.com/yarrowkat.

Other Poetry by Echobird Press

The Gatekeeper Wears Acrylics by Court Winterborne
the bones of this land by Kat Heatherington
No Longer Water by Katrina Kaye

ECHOBIRD
PRESS

Fiction by Echobird Press

Friends With Wings by Maxwell Pearl
The Alters series by Terra Katherine McKeown